PARENTING AMONG
# CHRISTIAN IMMIGRANTS
## IN THE UNITED STATES

# PARENTING AMONG
# CHRISTIAN IMMIGRANTS
## IN THE UNITED STATES

Michael O. Akintayo Ph.D

Library of Congress Control Number:       2009909385
ISBN:            Hardcover                978-1-4415-7099-4
                 Softcover                978-1-4415-7098-7

This book was printed in the United States of America.

**To order additional copies of this book, contact:**
Xlibris Corporation
1-888-795-4274
www.Xlibris.com
Orders@Xlibris.com
66248

# CONTENTS

# DEDICATION

This book is dedicated to my parents Elder Joseph and Victoria Akintayo, my wife Funke Akintayo, my children-Tolulope Ajiboye, Tokunbo, Tinuke, Tolani, Michael Jr (MJ); my siblings Pastor Abayomi, Temitope, Pastor Ayokunnu and Anuoluwa Akintayo.

# ACKNOWLEDGEMENTS

I THANK GOD Almighty, who has sustained me to stand every storm that came along my path in pursuit of knowledge and excellence. It is He who has given me the strength to be hopeful in times of troubles, trials, and tribulations while working on my doctoral degree and most importantly on this book. I will forever appreciate His goodness, love and care for helping me to reach this stage.

I would not have realized my dreams if not for my parents. This medium cannot express my heartfelt appreciation to both of you for believing in me and for having the strong faith that I could do it. I gratefully appreciate you for giving me education as an inheritance that can never be taken away from me. The childhood education and effective upbringing you instilled in me led to who I am today, and your actions are commendable.

Along with my parents and my siblings and other noble people whom I call my family, to those who have passed on to Glory (Dr. Osuolale Osunleke, Mr & Mrs Akintade, Christiana Oyebanji, Akintunde Akintayo and Chief Olusola Bilewu), I thank God for your lives and wish you could have stayed longer to witness the publication of my first book, but it pleased God to take you away. To my siblings and other family members who are alive, I am so proud to be your uncle, brother, and cousin. I will always be grateful to all of you for your love.

I would like to extend my gratitude to my friends, coworkers, choir members, Board of Elders, Pastor Tunde Ogumyemi, Pastor Yinka Oderinde, Pastor Steven Onifade, Pastor Yemi Ayeni and Pastor Sunday Gbolagun of Christ Apostolic Church, international Miracle Center, Brooklyn, New York and my spiritual parents Prophet Dr. Samuel. K. and Christiana Abiara, of Christ Apostolic Church worldwide—The General Evangelist and Rev. David Adenodi (DGS). My career mentors—Dr. Charles Gray, Dr. Ishola Kokumo, Dr. Gregory Ajose, and Professor Allen Adeleke—for giving me the opportunity to have a new learning experience at Metropolitan College of New York. I thank all of you for providing the needed support to achieve my educational goal.

This book could not be complete without a reference to a critical time when all hope seemed to have been lost. My struggle, trial, and tribulations during that time encouraged me to become the best that I could be for my family, friends, myself, and, above all, to my creator. To people who have accepted me as their son–Elder and Mrs Samson Dada, Elder Ajao, Prince Gbadegesin and Esther Adeleye, (relocated to Nigeria), and my father in law, Bishop (Dr) Emmanuel Bilewu (JP), and Pastor Joseph Oyebanji. Thank you for your support.

A million thanks to my children—Tolulope Ajiboye, Tokunbo, Tinuke, Tolani, and Michael Jr.—and my wife (Funke) for their love, endurance, and understanding. Words cannot express my appreciation and love for you. My utmost goal to write this book would be impossible without your encouragement and support. Your endurance and commitment to my success are my source of inspiration and strength.

To Dr. Wendy Andberg, who worked tirelessly with me to get this far in my educational pursuit, I owe you a million thanks. I cannot put into words my appreciation to you for all you have done for me on this journey. You provided me your professional expertise and encouraged me to excel. I can not forget you and your husband Michael for being such good friends at the most turbulent times in my life.

To Dr. Ruth Bundy, Dr. Ayn Embar-Seddon and Dr. Edward Muldrow and Ms. Sue Browender at Capella University Minnesota and my editor Dr. Dave Healy (Minnesota) who gave me hope, encouragement and support that made my doctoral degree and the completion of this book possible. He also worked tirelessly on the manuscript. I owe you a big thank you. You will always be acknowledged in my career. Thank you for your guidance and support. To the entire staff of Met Council on Jewish Poverty especially Ms. Ruth Turshen and Ilene Marcus, without you there will be no MAICO NY Inc. Thank you very much from the bottom of my heart. Above all, the completion of this book is neither by might or power, but to God Almighty that I owe everything.

# CHAPTER 1

# INTRODUCTION

I N RECENT YEARS, the number of immigrants entering the United States has increased, and many wonder about the effects of migration on issues like parenting, marriage and family, and divorce. In this book, my main focus will be on Christian parenting among immigrants in America, acknowledging various studies to show the significance of this topic. Immigrants are people who move from one nation to another with the intention that the move be permanent. The decision to move often depends on an individual, with the intention that the decision will improve family social status and provide better employment and educational opportunities.

Studies of immigrant families show that conflicts between parents and their second-generations adolescents are pretty intense when compared to conflict with first-generation children and nonimmigrant populations. Research has shown also that adolescents from disrupted families tend not to do well in school. They are more likely to become delinquent, drop out, and experience depression. What I am trying to say is that raising your children must be your priority as you live in this unique environment.

Parenting is a challenging task that puts responsibilities on parents, guardians, or other adults to take care of and nurture their children to become productive and responsible citizens. It is the primary responsibility of parents to raise responsible adults, especially in a world full of corruption, immorality, and indiscipline. In a world that encourages young children not to listen to voices that promote biblical principles, parents cannot but worry about the future of their children. It is the responsibility of parents to instruct and discipline their children.

When we instruct our children, we are encouraging them to follow certain standards or guidelines. God's guidelines supersede others, and parents must guide, direct, and instruct their children in God's way. Jesus told Peter that upon this mountain I will build my church. Parents, you need to build your family upon a solid foundation by training your children, using the appropriate tools and skills given to you by God. You need to mobilize and enhance your parenting skills to suit this environment. God expects you to be responsible for your children in this country. Make God your solid foundation upon which you raise your children.

As Christians, when we instruct our children we are teaching them to follow the precepts or standards of God. It is a training that shows how our children should act according to the ordinances of God so they can make correct decisions. They are taught to be responsible for their actions or decisions, and it is a life-long process that may entail discipline of our children whenever necessary. Remember, Psalm 127:3 says that children are a gift from the LORD; they are a reward from Him. Parents are to show and demonstrate love to their children. I notice that many of our immigrant parents love their children unconditionally, but sometimes some of us do not know how to show that we love them.

Too often, our definition of love is about buying expensive gifts like name-brand shoes, clothes, and cars. A friend of mine shared his experience with me. He said that for many years his children lived with his parents, and he made a vow that he would not allow distance to be a barrier between him and the children. Therefore, he made sure that he called his children at least twice a day, almost everyday. By the time the left his homeland, they were very used to him. His children's birthdays, graduation, or Christmas never passed without a call from him. Apart from sending them to prestigious private school in his country, he made sure that they were involved in the decisions he made.

Another friend explained to me that she makes sure that her children feel her presence in the house every time she comes home from work. She asks them about their daily activities in school and sits with them to complete their homework. She said that her children are doing well in school and they attribute that to her role as a parent. What I am saying is that there are many ways you can express your love to your children, depending on your situation. The function of a family is to raise a child to have healthy relationships. This includes raising children in a loving and supportive environment, pleasing to God so that they can develop their knowledge and values, and behave in an appropriate and acceptable manner in society.

## Sense of Purpose

The purpose of my book is to facilitate an understanding of parenting among immigrants in the United States because many views are out there about the relationships between parenting and social problems like youth violence, child abuse, and adolescent social problems. This book addresses some of the concerns of immigrant parents as they raise their children and young adults in the United States. It explores different parenting beliefs among immigrant populations and provides coping strategies that can assist these parents in parenting their children and young adults effectively in America.

According to Migration Information Source (2002), foreign-born Africans make up 3% of the total foreign-born population of the United States. Of the 33 million foreign-born people in the United States in 2002, 1 million, or 3%, were from Africa. Additionally, the American Community Survey (2002) found that, of foreign-born Africans, Nigerians living in the United States were by far the largest group, numbering 139,500, compared to 108,000 Egyptians, 87,500 Ethiopians, and 70,000 South Africans.

Also, over the last three decades many Latinos—Mexicans, Puerto Ricans, Cubans, Central Americans, South Americans, and other ethnic groups—have immigrated to the United States, while the population of second-generation (children and young adults born in the United States with at least one foreign-born parent) is increasing rapidly. Therefore, it is important to discuss sensitive topics like parenting and other issues—values, language, assimilation, acculturation—as they affect how children and young adults are raised in the United States.

Becoming a parent is a transition that requires new roles and responsibilities. New parents sometimes feel overwhelmed with the arrival of a new family member because it complicates their existing relationship. This book will describe the experiences of immigrant parents as they raise their children and young adults in the United States. The book will also inform you about challenges for parents in this country and measures necessary to raise children and young adults so that they can become productive, responsible, and God-fearing adults.

This book explores the challenges of parenting that immigrants face in a new culture and the extent to which American values have affected their parenting practices. This exploration may improve relationships between immigrant parents and their young adult offspring, as well as those who come in contact with them. My passion to write a book on parenting among immigrants stems from my personal experiences working with immigrant youth. I have seen newly arrived young adults and children disrespecting their parents, skipping classes, and doing things without parental consent. They talk back to their parents and try to prove that they can do anything and get away with it.

I have seen kids exercising authority over their immigrant parents, perhaps because they realize that their parents are not legal residents of this country, or because they think they know a lot about the American system. They want their parents to attend to them on their own terms. As a result, I see that these parents are frustrated, embarrassed, and depressed. It is not pleasant to see parents lose control or authority over their children. Our children are supposed to be our joy, especially for Christian immigrant parents. As immigrant parents, most of us assume that our traditions, values, and customs are enough to make our children become responsible and respectful, but many parents often find this does not happen. I hope this book helps immigrant parents realize the need to effectively raise their children and young adults in the United States. I also hope that this book will assist in improving their parenting skills and practices.

# CHAPTER 2

# PARENTING AND DIVERSITY

I N THIS SECTION, my intention is to describe parenting among immigrant populations in general. I will briefly discuss parenting values and practices in order to show that many immigrant populations have similar ways of raising their children and young adults. I will start with the Hispanic population.

## *Hispanic–Latinos*

These are people who originate from the Spanish-speaking countries of Latin America. They are also referred to as *Latinos*, people of Spanish and Indian background "whose ancestors have always lived in areas of Southwest United States that were once part of Mexico" (Fonte, 2002, p. 31). For example, many Latinos or Hispanics identify themselves by their national origin as Dominicans, Mexicans, etc. In 2001, the U.S. Census Bureau indicated that Hispanics are one of the fastest-growing immigrant populations, making up more than 12% of the U.S population.

Like every immigrant population, Hispanics are a heterogeneous group, and individual Latinos in America may accept or reject certain traditional parenting customs and values. Like every other immigrant population in the United States, most Latino parents are raising wonderful and loving families without serious problems. Hispanics value close family relationships, or *familismo*. This term signifies a sense of deep family responsibility, which includes respect for one's elders and a desire to care for all members and protect them.

For Latinos, their source of joy and pride is their family. Hispanic parents will do positive things to ensure that their children are not disrespectful. They strive to teach their children to behave well in public, with or without their parents. Latino children are instructed to follow orders and show loyalty to the family. Like most immigrant parents, Latinos are strict and authoritarian when it comes to disciplining their children. However, times are changing, and many Latinos are trying to be authoritative parents, shifting from corporal punishment to parenting that promotes positive relationships with their children and young adults. One way some parents have done this is by living in Latino communities in the United States so as to generate greater support and resources for raising their children.

## Africa

Parenting in Africa rests on the belief that values are learned within the family and passed from generation to generation. Values are transmitted through proverbs and stories by community leaders, elders, and family members, who also help to instill them during holidays and special gatherings or celebrations (McGoldrick, 2005). Traditional religious beliefs play significant roles in the lives of Africans. Parenting in Africa involves teaching the young to believe in the power of both natural and spiritual worlds (Mbiti, cited in McGoldrick). During childhood, Africans learn that each African country has its own religious system, and the people worship a Supreme God, divinities, spirits, and ancestors.

Spirituality and spiritual beliefs are among the core values of parenting in Africa. African children and young adults are taught to believe in the existence of spirits in nonliving things: rocks, mountains, and rivers. This forms the basis of their religious expression through mystic powers, magic, and witchcraft—notions clearly at odds with Western religion (Oyeshile, 2003).

As with most immigrants, parenting among Africans focuses on community identity. Community is important because it is considered the source of spiritual identity (McGoldrick, 2005). Africans are taught to engage relatives and friends in planning celebrations of births, marriages, and funerals. African parents dedicate time to teach their children about their cultural history and traditions. Children learn the values of family, marriage, and rituals through vital means such as plays and observations (Kamya, 2005; McGoldrick, 2005).

MICHAEL O. AKINTAYO PH.D

African children and young adults are raised to appreciate and understand the importance of kin relationships beyond ties of marriage and blood to include other members of their tribe (Fadipe, cited in McGoldrick, 2005). African tribes speak different languages, and each tribe shares a unique history and social and political organization (McGoldrick). Once a child is born into a tribe, the child remains a member forever. Hospitality is one of the powerful facets of life in Africa. Like many immigrant children, children are raised to be respectful and hospitable to peers, adults, and visitors. Any experiences that challenge these values and practices may lead to punishment and psychological distress (Kamya, 2005; McGoldrick).

African children learn early that men are the heads of families, with major responsibilities to manage and direct family affairs, settle misunderstandings, and supervise major events (Fadipe, cited in McGoldrick, 2005). In Africa, fathers appoint the oldest son to be the heir, whereas women are in charge of birth rituals. Also, women serve as caregivers for children and the elderly. In Africa, the birth of a child is welcomed with excitement and a big celebration by the family members. Names of newborn children reflect the events that surround their births (Mbiti, cited in McGoldrick).

## Nigeria

The United Nations estimated that the population of Nigeria in 2004 was 150 million, making it the most populous country in Africa (Soyinka-Airewelle, 2003). Nigeria comprises about 250 ethnic groups with thousands of languages (Adeyanju, 2000; Osundeko, 2006). The name *Yoruba* or *Yarriba* means "cunning" and is an alias given to the Yoruba people by their neighbors, the Hausa-Fulani in the northern part of Nigeria. Yoruba-speaking people are found in southwestern Nigeria (Airewelle, 2003; Soyinka, 2003).

Religion plays a vital role among Nigerian Yoruba families because they believe in the Supreme Being as their guidance. Traditional Nigerian Yoruba parents practice several religions, but recently, many have converted to Islam and Christianity and few practice African traditional religion

(Adeyanju, 2000). The Supreme God is known as *Olodumare*, the creator, and is considered omnipotent and righteous. For the Yoruba, one's conduct in life must align with the dictates of Olodumare (Oyeshile, 2003). Predestination is also central to the values of the Nigerian Yoruba. This belief sees a person's destiny, successes, and failures as predetermined from birth. Before a child is born, an oracle will be consulted to find out about his or her future and the appropriate way to raise the child (Dixey, 1999).

The traditional Yoruba family consists of kinship (extended family) known as *idile*, described by Adeyanju (2000) as people who share the same ancestors with people of the extended family. Nigerian Yoruba consider all adults in their *idile* as biological parents because they are collectively responsible for effective parenting. In traditional Yoruba culture, cousins, nieces, and nephews are not distinguished; all are regarded as birth children. However, distinctions are made between older and younger siblings (Adeyanju, 2000; Osundeko, 2006). Ogunnaike (1997) observed that the older siblings often take on the responsibility of caring for and nurturing their younger siblings early in life—a particularly difficult practice to maintain in Western culture.

Nigerian Yoruba culture values men as heads of households who wield enormous responsibility in decision making, whereas Yoruba mothers are also important in the affairs of a child but do not make final decisions. When it comes to making an important decision about a child, the mother leaves the final decision to the father (Osundeko, 2006), but for the most part childrearing is a joint effort between Nigerian Yoruba parents. However, they may find it difficult to understand the principle of joint custody since in their culture a father is believed to "own" a child (Osundeko, 2006).

Children and young adults are socialized to show respect to their elders (Osundeko, 2006). Children are raised to uphold central moral and social norms, including *iwa* (character). A person who is well-behaved is said to have iwa, and a morally upright person is known as *omoluwabi*. *Iwaburuku*, on the other hand, refers to undesirable moral conduct (Oyeshile, 2003).

Traditional Yoruba parents believe that communal responsibility allows a child to acquire family values and beliefs, which is important because the child is regarded as the ambassador of the family to the whole world (Moleye, 1999). Yoruba parents wish to be well-represented in public by their children. This is portrayed by the Yoruba saying "Omo eni iba joni a ba yo" ("It will be worthy of celebration if one's child alters one's ego") (Moleye, 1999).

Emphasis is placed on raising a child who will perpetuate traditions with proper manners. Among the Ondo people of the Yoruba ethnic group, the idea of *omolere* indicates a worthy ambassador (Moleye, 1999).

Many Africans believe that child care and parenting of young adult offspring is not the responsibility of biological parents alone. Friends, family members, and the extended family are actively involved in taking care of Yoruba children and young adults.

In Africa, traditional culture is passed on through informal, rather than formal, education. Children and young adults are made to understand that they are loved but cannot misbehave. Any misconduct is met with corporal punishment or other forms of discipline so that children and young adults are aware of the implications of bad behavior (Ogunaike, 1997; Osundeko, 2006).

Yoruba parents educate their children to be responsible because parenting is seen as purposeful. Among traditional Yoruba parents, it is a valued opportunity to have children who will live long enough to bury their parents. Traditional Yoruba parenting practices emphasize respect, obedience, and the use of physical discipline (Moleye, 1999).

# CHAPTER 3

# PERSONAL REFLECTIONS

TO PARENT EFFECTIVELY means to adopt God's standards to develop our children so they can be empowered to be self-sufficient. Proverbs 22:6 refers to the importance of biblical parenting: "Train a child in the way he should go, and when he is old he will not turn from it." As Christians our children should be our priority. God expects us to parent them according to His teachings. Therefore, parents need to pray for wisdom, peace and tranquility, patience, and grace to be able to parent effectively.

Dr. John Wesley referred to parenting as the greatest challenge confronting Asian immigrants, especially those from strong Christian backgrounds. As I was growing up, the challenging task became obvious in many ways as my parents struggled to raise five young boys. Their moral commitment to the fulfillment of our social well-being was demonstrated by their commitment to raise us in Christian ways with Pentecostal beliefs and values.

My parents knew that their spiritual responsibilities were aligned with their parenting practices. My parents were teachers who would not accept inappropriate behavior from their children. They were disciplinarians but loving. We had a schedule for studying, for lunch, for socializing, and every night one of us would read the Bible and my father would share a message from the Bible reading and pray with us before we went to bed. My parents were God-fearing and wanted to raise their children with biblical principles. They wanted us to be devoted Christians. I grew up seeing my father teaching Sunday school and sometimes preaching before he became an elder. Until this very day my father will not miss a prayer or worship meeting for anything.

Sometimes in the evening, my mother would entertain us by singing some of her favorite hymns: *I have found a friend in Jesus, He is everything to me, The Great physician now is here.* Some were in our Yoruba language:

*Yin Yin Ohun elo orin ati duru.* These are sprit-filled songs that inspire Christians to know and appreciate God. When school was in session, my parents required that we attend evening classes, and during school breaks we went to coaching school. The values that were important to them included teaching their children to know God, and to respect and love others.

My parents' style of raising us gave us a sense of responsibility that we must become reliable adults. This shows that parents and family are significant in shaping a child's behavior, attitudes, and personality. I believe it is helpful to discuss my childhood as an illustration of what follows in this book.

My father is an elder in the Christ Apostolic Church, in Ibadan, Oyo State, in Nigeria. Both of my parents spent many years in the church choir, and I later joined them in the choir, first singing alto and then tenor. My mother was one of the golden voices of CAC Church Irefin in Ibadan before my parents retired from the choir ministry. After many years my father was ordained as an elder.

Later, my brother joined me in the choir, and other siblings engaged themselves in different church activities. My parents made sure that all of us were doing something significant in the house of God. Did I mention that three of us were actually born in the church mission with a midwife and not at the hospital? That tells you how spiritual my parents were and still are. On many occasions, my brothers and I represented the children's ministry of my church in biblical contests among Christ Apostolic Churches in Ibadan, Oyo State, and won. One year after I became a member of the adult choir, my brother won the Presidential Award in a Bible contest among all Christ Apostolic Churches in Ibadan, at Liberty Stadium, Oyo State, Nigeria.

My parents did a wonderful job in providing us with a solid foundation as Christians. Before I left for college, I joined two other peers in assisting the church organist because we were sponsored to study music. What I learned during that time is still valuable today. I acknowledge the church and its contribution to my music career.

My parents taught my siblings and me to make education our priority. In fact, we couldn't have done otherwise because we saw how our parents trained each other all the way from elementary school to the University of Ibadan, where they both received their associate degrees in education. We knew that doing well in school was the right thing to do, before we would embark on other aspects of life. My parents struggled together and graduated from college after we had grown. Their personal lives are testimonies of hope, courage, love, and assurance that we could do it.

My parents admonished us to make education our best friend because it is the key to success. This prompted me to continue my education after I received my bachelor's degree in sociology from the University of Ibadan in Nigeria. I came to the United States and attended Metropolitan College of New York, formerly Audrey Cohen College, School of Human Services, where I obtained a master's degree in administration, specializing in human services. Later, I obtained advanced graduate certificates in online teaching and health care administration, and a Ph.D. in general human services specializing in family issues, nonprofit organizations, administration, ethnicity, and diversity from Capella University, in Minneapolis, Minnesota.

Today, my parents are proud parents of three young graduates with advanced degrees, one with a Higher National Diploma, while our youngest brother recently completed his Ordinary National Diploma in Nigeria. Two of my siblings are ordained pastors in Nigeria, working relentlessly to promote the work of God. What I am saying to all Christian immigrants is that our prayers and the time we spend teaching our children the word of God can inspire them to become responsible and reliable adults. When you show your children the right path, they will not depart from it.

Many immigrant parents are hard-working to the point that I wonder when they have time for their children. Sometimes, it takes the special grace of God for parents to slow down and think of retirement. Many immigrant parents are tireless and work graveyard shifts to provide for their children. This is an attempt to make sure their children are independent and self-sufficient. It is the responsibility of every parent, especially immigrant parents, to talk to their children about their careers and offer advice and information that can help them better prepare for the future.

Many immigrants left their home countries for the United States with a sense of purpose to provide a better life for their family. In the process, immigrant parents must carry their children along to fulfill this dream.

They should make sure that children take advantage of opportunities in the United States.

Living in America can be strenuous for immigrants. They must deal with acculturation, culture shock, and the fact that they may not be able to return to their home countries. Many immigrants have to work, take care of their family in the United States, take care of relatives back home, and deal with prejudice and racism.

Many immigrant parents put in long hours at work and do their best to provide for their family, but still barely make ends meet. Many do not have adequate time with their children, resulting in a lack of intimacy between them and their children. Parents can easily be overwhelmed and confused.

Sociologists have described the family as a system of roles with significant expectations for behavior. The family is also seen as a social institution through which children develop norms, values, and roles that lead to socialization. This makes parenting one of the most important functions of the family. Parents are expected to provide love, acceptance, warmth, and peace for the development of their children.

Many immigrant parents in the United States aspire to raise responsible citizens while they adapt to parenting practices of the host country. However, they are faced with numerous challenges—immigration, acculturation, economic hardship, lack of employment, and literacy—that make parenting very difficult. Despite these challenges, most immigrant parents cherish the values of respect, hard work, honesty, and mild discipline when raising their children and young adults in a host country like America.

## Increased Opportunities

Many immigrant parents describe the United States as a land of opportunity and say they are able to provide a better life here for their families. Bacallao and Smokowski (2007) interviewed Mexican families to find out why they immigrated to the United States. Two primary reasons were given: First, they thought better job opportunities existed in the United States to support their family. Second, they immigrated to seek a better future for their children. Some parents were especially impressed by the number of colleges in the United States. They have taken advantage of scholarships, grants, and loans. They praised the potential of technology for facilitating school work and for connecting them to their children when they are not together.

# CHAPTER 4

# PARENTING STRUGGLE
# OF IMMIGRANTS

I N MY EXPERIENCE with immigrants, I have heard many stories of how they managed to get to the United States. An especially interesting one was told by my friend from Liberia, Rev. Wahynoh Gbofeh. He graduated from the University of Liberia to become a teacher and vice principal in his home country. He left his wife and two children in Liberia to come to America to improve his life, hoping that one day they could join him.

He started his new life by doing odd jobs: working in a factory moving boxes, cleaning houses, and working as a security officer. After many years, he got his green card, brought his family to the United States, attended a seminary and obtained his master's degree, worked at a hospital, for private companies, and for New York City. He became an adjunct professor and a pastor who now has a church and a nonprofit organization that helps teenagers become responsible adults. He said that what really helped him is that he is married to a woman who was raised with the fear of God. Her parents taught her to be a woman of substance. He said that he is happy that he has a happy family. What a remarkable and successful story of an American dreamer.

Another friend—Niyi, a Nigerian—left his home country after graduating from college and serving his country for a year. He first went to Europe, where he worked on tomato farms and later with a construction company. He saved enough money to take care of his parents back home, which enabled them to retire.

He eventually left Europe with $3,500 in his pocket, arriving in the Bahamas, where he and a friend spent three weeks. One night they were robbed at gun point by local thugs, and most of their money was taken. With difficulty, they made it to Florida.

On his first night in the United States, Niyi tried to call an uncle, but the uncle's phone had been disconnected. Eventually he got through and was able to get the phone number of his secondary school teacher, who was then living in the Bronx. The man was not home, but his wife answered, and she told Niyi and his friend to come and stay with them.

Niyi stayed with this wonderful, God-fearing family for eleven months. He described them as the epitome of simplicity, genuine love, hospitality, and wisdom. They took care of him and his friend as if they were their own children. Niyi recalled the day he announced that he was going to leave rent an apartment. It was a difficult move because the family did not want him to leave.

Four years later, Niyi married a middle-class woman whose parents had no time to raise her and her siblings. Both parents pursued their own careers at the expense of raising their children, although they did provide for them financially. The woman Niyi married graduated from one of the best colleges in the United States, but her family life was marked by turmoil and selfishness.

Niyi learned the hard way how important it is for parents to provide a good example for their children. His mother-in-law eventually encouraged her daughter to file for divorce. Niyi asked the judge if they could go for counseling, but the mother-in-law resisted that suggestion. She even lied that Niyi's children had been forcibly sent to their country to live with his parents, when in fact that decision had been a joint one by everyone involved. Finally, after months of sleepless nights, anxiety, depression, and uncertainty, he was exonerated.

Niyi said his ex-wife did nothing to maintain contact with their children while they were in their country. Even on Christmas, Thanksgiving, or their birthdays, he had to call her and remind her to call the children. After many years, the in-laws kidnapped the children from his parents and took them to an unknown destination for six months before bringing them to the United States.

I heard another immigration story from a West African woman. Usually it is men who come to the United States and leave their families behind, but in her case she was the one to make that move. She was working for an airline company in Ghana and was able to get a visa to come to America. After several months she got a job as a domestic worker and assumed responsibility of providing for her children and husband back home.

This woman did not become a legal resident for eight years. By the time she visited Ghana, her husband had established a second family. She then brought her children to the United States and raised them as a single parent, an experience she described as "hell."

Her children wanted to be like Americans. They were bullied in school and had few friends. She said, "Sometimes they would refuse to do what I ask them to do and I had no father figure for them to turn to." What sustained her through this difficult experience was her faith in God, which she tried to instill in her children as well.

Another friend, who is Costa Rican, came to the United States ten years ago. He was a medical doctor in his home country but could not practice here because he did not pass the board examination. He was reduced to doing odd jobs to survive. During this time, he was unable to visit his family in Costa Rica, and his relationship with them suffered.

After many years, he brought his children to the U.S. and found out that it did not take long before they began to adopt American values and behavior. He said it was a constant struggle to make his children keep their traditional values. To his disappointment, the children did not want to speak Spanish among their peers. His native language is very important to him, and he wants his children to maintain it.

To those parents and children in a similar situation, my suggestion is that this issue be handled with patience, love, and respect. Children, love your parents, respect them, and be patient with them, even when they do not understand why you don't want to speak your native language. See if you can reach a compromise. Parents should understand that American culture encourages clear communication, where children are allowed to express their feelings.

# CHAPTER 5

# CHALLENGES OF IMMIGRANT PARENTS

IMMIGRANT FAMILIES WANT to provide a better life for their children. When immigrants arrive in the United States, they tend to settle among their own people, where they feel more comfortable and secure. However, that may not help them with one of their biggest challenges: learning English. With limited English skills, getting a good job is impossible, as is helping their children with school work. Forced to take jobs with no medical benefits, many immigrants experience poor health. They also face discrimination and racism.

Perhaps the biggest challenge immigrants face as parents is adapting their cultural values, beliefs, and parenting practices to their host country. Children of immigrants typically want to be treated as Americans, and they may not share their parents' sense of importance about retaining their native language. They do not want to be raised the way their parents were raised.

In a new country, both parents and children are subject to the forces of acculturation, which leads them to accept the cultural values of the dominant society (Kamya, 2005; Martinez, 1988). Often, immigrants are caught between the cultural values and practices of their country of origin and those of their new country. This causes many tensions, but especially in the area of parenting.

My experience working with immigrants has shown me that in the United States young adults have too much freedom, and this sometimes becomes a challenge for parents. For example, Maria said, "The way they behave in school, they want to bring it in the house in the United States. I do not tolerate this with my kids." James complained that older children "tend to shift the responsibility to the younger ones." Victoria, a Nigerian with five children, observed that in Nigeria "you are not legally an adult until you are 21, and even so, culturally, if you're living with your parents at or after 21 years, you're not totally independent. You have to listen to your parents and obey them."

In describing the effects of external influences on children in the United States, the Nigerian parents I interviewed mostly mentioned negative ones. Mary cited the deleterious consequences of one-parent families, as well as the pernicious influence of drugs. Jose lamented that "in this country when parents do something that is displeasing to a young adult, he/she takes them to court." James complained about the prevalence of profanity, while Mary expressed her distaste for men wearing earrings and for low-riding pants. Ade suggested that the American emphasis on material possessions subverts young adults' attention to their education.

Research suggests that most immigrant parents want to maintain their cultural values, traditions, and language in their new country (Chao & Tseng, 2002). Immigrant parents often express concern about keeping their culture alive by teaching children their religious traditions, mode of dress, and language. I agree that immigrant parents need to transmit their beliefs in God and the value of respect and education, as well as the importance of obedience and living a moral life.

The challenges of parenting in the United States are summed up in differing attitudes about respect. For instance, calling elderly people by their name is not acceptable in Yoruba culture (a group of people from Nigeria, to which I belong). Prostrating or bowing down and kneeling (for girls) is an aspect of Yoruba culture that most young adults resist. Among traditional Latino families, *respeto* for parents and older family members, along with obedience and politeness, are core values (National Campaign, 2008).

Some parents believe, as the Bible teaches, that children should honor their parents, but they find that for their young adult offspring, respect and obedience are not automatic in America. As Ade noted, "In the United States, you have to keep reminding them to do house chores. Young adults in New York seem to be lazy to do normal duty in the house."

American law is perceived as a challenge to parenting among Nigerian Yoruba. They see the government here as having considerable influence on how parents raise their young adults, unlike in Nigeria, where parents have full rights to raise their children however they want. Parents describe themselves as busier with their jobs here than in Nigeria, making it more difficult to balance their work and home lives. They lament their diminished ability to oversee what their children do and the kind of friends they keep. And they feel more alone as American parents who lack the social resources of a society in which it takes a village to raise a child.

MICHAEL O. AKINTAYO PH.D

# CHAPTER 6

# INDIVIDUALISM AND COLLECTIVISM PARADIGMS

TWO PARADIGMS (WAYS of thinking) have been used to explain how parents raise their children in a new environment. First is the paradigm of individualism, which is an egocentric way of single-handedly or independently raising children without external support. Parents in Western Europe and United States tend to be individualistic in raising their children, and children in turn are encouraged to pursue individual goals.

Under the individualistic paradigm, children are taught to get what they want without regard for who is left behind in the process. Individualistic parenting emphasizes that children should be responsible for themselves and become whatever they aspire to become by themselves. Children raised under this parenting practice learn early in life that they need to be proactive and aggressive to become successful.

The second paradigm, collectivism, is commonly found among traditional Africans, Latin Americans, and Asians. Collectivism is a parenting practice involving communal or joint efforts in raising children to benefit the parents and their loved ones, as well as society in general. Many immigrant parents from Africa, Latin America, and Asia are used to the parenting practices of collectivism, where extended family members take part in raising children. An uncle or aunt, or even a close friend, can discipline your children when they act inappropriately in public because parenting is considered a joint effort.

Parents who practice this type of parenting believe in the notion of "we" or "togetherness." It is an exhibition of harmony and loyalty while raising their children to become responsible. These parents raise their children to be supportive of their family and avoid public confrontation. They consider public confrontation and inappropriate behavior as a disgrace or embarrassment to the entire family. In a collectivist society, parents raise their children to express their disagreement in a dignified way.

When people raised in a collectivist society arrive in the United States, they often appear to natives as indirect or not straightforward. Others may think they have something to hide. A friend of mine had this problem when he arrived here. His ex-sister-in-law thought he had something to hide because my friend would rarely look at others when speaking or being spoken to. To complicate matters, he found it difficult to say no to his ex-sister-in-law's demands. My friend is a warm, kind, and wonderful person, but he still had to battle his upbringing upon arrival in the United States.

The more successful parents are at socializing their children into family norms and values, the less control will be necessary in raising them in a new culture or environment. In every society, effective parenting involves effective communication. This brings hope, love, and endurance to individual members of the family and brings the family closer together.

Immigrant parents must balance their traditional patterns of parenting with the expectations and demands of a new society. Many immigrant parents struggle to let go of the traditional ways, while adjusting how they raise their children and young adults in a new environment. Children may believe that their parents think less of them when they attempt to become more independent. My advice to immigrant parents is to negotiate conflicts with your children in such a way that you demonstrate your love and care for them.

Many immigrant parents acknowledge that they have adapted their traditional parenting practices since coming to the United States. Interestingly, some parents started this process before leaving their home countries, where they allowed their children to wear Western clothes and watch American and European movies. Many of them realized that traditional ways of discipline would not be accepted in American society.

To understand how their children and young adults can best develop, immigrant parents must examine their children's social relationships: their friends and the different groups they belong to. These relationships, if healthy, can serve as an important support system for the primary family relationship.

# CHAPTER 7

# THEORETICAL FRAMEWORK

S OCIAL SYSTEMS THEORY (Bentalanffy, cited in Perry & Perry, 2006), ecological theory (Bronfenbrenner, cited in Dale, Smith, Norlin, & Chess, 2006), and cultural variant theory (Allen, 1978) served as the theoretical foundations for developing this book. These theories helped me understand the perceptions of immigrant parents regarding their parenting styles and practices, beliefs, and challenges they face while raising their children and young adult offspring in the United States. This chapter provides brief discussions of these theories.

## Social Systems Theory

Bertalanffy has been described as the father of general systems. According to Bertalanffy (cited in Perry & Perry, 2006), social systems theory is a collection of interacting individuals who can be better understood within the context of their physical and social environments. For example, perceptions of parenting among specific immigrant parents in the United States can be better understood in light of their present geographical structure and social environment (Longress, 2000).

According to Longress (2000), the smallest social system consists of two individuals (dyad), whereas complex systems are triads or larger and include groups such as families and community organizations. Social systems theory suggests that individuals in social systems are bound by a common identity that distinguishes them from outsiders. Individual family members have roles and statuses based on authority and traditions that serve as a family culture. Interactions that occur in a human system are dynamic and transactional. Changes in interactions within social systems depend on the situations in which individual members find themselves.

Dale, Smith, Norlin, and Chess (2006) defined interactional transactions as those involving face-to-face contact. Among young adults, interactions occurring in primary groups establish identity and personality. Such groups include friends, family, community members, religious groups, ethnic groups, and nations.

Corey (2005) suggested that social systems theory can be used to understand families because it can stimulate new research and provide an in-depth understanding of child development, adult adaptation, and the development of close relationships. The influence of social systems theory is evident in work by sociologists such as Cottrell, as well as family therapists—notably Ackerman, Jackson, Haley, and Weakland, who emphasized different communication models within the family (Corey, 2005). Minuchin's structural approach is another systemic perspective that emphasizes the importance of the family and the regulation of its boundaries as an institution (cited in Dale et al., 2006).

Individuals and families are part of larger social systems (Andersen, Carter, & Lowe, 2006; Parke, 2004). In the early 1900s, theorists such as Sigmund Freud believed that understanding human behavior was best done by focusing on individual internal attributes (Berk, 2006). In the early 1940s, both natural and social scientists began to understand the importance of interrelationships in ecological systems.

Social systems theory perceives the family as a complex and integrated whole (Minuchin, 2007). Individual members are part of the family and of the larger society. Individual family members cannot be understood independently because a family includes smaller subunits that involve relationships between husband and wife, parents and children, and siblings with each other. The subsystems or subunits of the family are defined by boundaries that must be clear and flexible for effective parenting (Andersen et al., 2006).

The fact that the family is a unit does not mean that we cannot focus on one or more of its subsystems, such as parents. The parental entity is a subsystem of the family that is worthy of understanding so that we can enhance family stability. Parents must be able to access external resources for the family's well-being, and siblings must be able to receive support from their parents when necessary (Minuchin, 2007; Olson & Defrain, 2006). Many studies have examined various

MICHAEL O. AKINTAYO PH.D

subsystems in the family in order to understand the functioning of the family as a macro system.

Andersen et al. (2006) focused on the behavioral aspects of social systems theory, which include social control and socialization, communication, and adaptation. Parental control may exist in the form of persuasion or coercion. External organizations may serve as support systems for or controls on parental behavior. Andersen et al. referred to socialization as a form of control that helps integrate individuals into the social system. From a micro perspective, the social systems may be family, church, mosque, community, or society. The main function of socialization is to accomplish the goals of the family as a system. The more successful parents are at socializing their children into family norms, values, practices, and culture, the less control will be necessary in raising their children in a new culture.

Another aspect of social systems theory that informs parenting is communication. Effective communication conveys hope, love, warmth, and endurance to individual members of the family and brings the family closer together (Andersen et al., 2006). For effective parenting to occur, parents must communicate effectively with family members, and it must be interactive (Olson & Defrain, 2006).

Another useful component of social systems theory to illuminate parenting is adaptation, which consists of both assimilation and accommodation. Adaptation is an important family function that involves responding to social change. Another function of adaptation is to enable family members to adjust to external stress experienced by individual members (Andersen et al., 2006).

Adaptation among immigrant parents will have much to do with adjusting to the host country. In the host country, immigrant parents may find it difficult to adapt to the dominant group while raising their children and young adult offspring. Applying social systems theory, Longress (2000) suggested that the extent to which parents overcome parenting challenges will be determined by the love and affection they have for their children and young adult offspring, which in turn can be affected by their access to economic and social resources.

Social systems theory is useful in evaluating the structures that people use to provide order and give meaning to their experience. Porpora (1989) applied Gidden's notion of structure to institutions such as courts, schools, and hospitals, concluding that a behavior such as parenting is influenced by such institutions, as well as by developmental issues and social forces. But the effect of all this is not monolithic. Instead, individuals make unique, subjective decisions based on their emotions and their experiences (Berk, 2006). Andersen et al. (2006) observed that social systems theory sees the family as a pattern of relationships of stability, social force, and change. Healey (2006) stated that the way individuals interact with one another defines their identities.

Parenting behavior, like human behavior in general, is influenced both by institutions and by individual personality. Immigrant parents must balance their institutionalized patterns of behavior with the expectations and demands of a new society. Many immigrant parents struggle as they try to let go of old patterns, adjusting how they raise their children while still holding onto traditional social roles (Dale et al., 2006).

Immigrant children and young adults may believe their parents think less of them when they express a desire to become more independent. Parents in turn may sense a need to adjust their responsibilities and rights while raising young adults in the United States (Dale et al., 2006). This may mean modifying the traditional hierarchical family structure. In a new environment like the United States, effective family functioning requires boundaries that are clear but flexible (Minuchin, 2007). Children and young adults must learn to negotiate misunderstandings or conflicts without constant interference from their parents but while still sensing their support (Minuchi; Olson & Defrain).

## Ecological Theory

Ecological theory is similar to social systems theory in its emphasis on the interrelationships of organisms with one another and with their environment (Bronfenbrenner, cited in Dale et al., 2006). Ecological theory maintains that human beings can be understood best within the context of where they live. For example, parenting among immigrant families can be best understood based on their experiences living in the United States. The relationship between people and their environment is reciprocal.

MICHAEL O. AKINTAYO PH.D

Ecological theory distinguishes among four types of systems: (a) micro-systems, (b) meso-systems, (c) exo-systems, and (d) macro-systems (Bronfenbrenner, cited in Longress, 2006; Osundeko, 2006). The core value of the micro-system is the direct contact that exists among individual members, demonstrating that people do not live in isolation. The micro-system involves activities and relationships within an individual's immediate surroundings: home, peer group, and school. Meso-systems are personal networks that people build for themselves. Exo-systems are institutions that influence one's micro-system. Macro-systems consist of the environment that hosts the first three systems. They include historical events and the broader culture. Macro-systems consist of cultural values, laws, and customs (Berk, 2007).

Bronfenbrenner (cited in Osundeko, 2006) noted that ecological or environmental forces affect parenting in many ways. In response to cultural attitudes in their host country, immigrant parents may modify their roles to provide some freedom for their young adult offspring, depending on the situation. This helps explain why sometimes the same parenting practice among different immigrant populations might lead to different developmental outcomes (Melendez, 2005).

Kelly (2006) considered parenting from an eco-cultural developmental context that includes parental expectations, disciplinary practices, beliefs about gender roles, religious and spiritual values, and child-rearing goals. Ecological theory (Ahmed & Lemkau, 2000; Bronfenbrenner, 2005; Jack, 2000) emphasizes the impact of macro-systems—for example, how immigrant parents' attachment to their home countries might affect how they raise their young adult offspring in a new environment. Many immigrants have been brought up in a society that instills the idea of a home country as the central point to which one must return (Sudarkasa, cited in McGoldrick, 2005). Many parents visit their home countries regularly with their young adults for special events such as festivals and ceremonies. In addition, many young adults are affected by the historical experiences, beliefs, and values of their parents. Other persistent influences include social-ethical beliefs, communal values, and religion—all of which influence the way traditional parents raise their children. These values include an emphasis on character, respect, opposition to selfishness, tolerance, and being pleasing to God.

Social systems theory and ecological theory help explain how immigrant parents raise their young adult offspring while they live in the United States. Parents develop their own parenting theory based on their cultural and group socialization, as well as individual and family experiences, personality style, and the characteristics of their children. As a result of cultural diversity in the United States, there is a plethora of beliefs and values regarding parenting. Therefore, there is need to discuss a third theory: cultural variant theory.

## Cultural Variant Theory

Nobles (1978, 1981) was a leading pioneer of the concept of Africanity, which is an example of cultural variant theory. According to this theory, an African cultural disposition is the basis of Black family life. Noble posited that Black family relationships are based on a sense of history, family, and a supreme power (God). Peterson (1986) elaborated on the three senses as follows:

1.  The sense of history connects Black family to their roots, which includes African heritage and the shared experience of racism and oppression.
2.  The sense of family equips members with an understanding that their identity and being rests upon the family, which serves as a social network of support, strength, protection, and unconditional love for its members.
3.  The sense of Supreme Being connects Black family members to the supreme force that guides them and enables to do things beyond their own limitations.

The cultural variant perspective accepts some family dynamics as universal but stresses that it is inappropriate for White family norms to justify what is normal or adaptive in Black families or vice versa (Allen, 1978). Peterson (1986) noted that families from different cultural backgrounds vary in their structural characteristics and functioning, arguing that one cannot understand the behavior of a person without understanding the specific cultural norms or rules that govern the behavior of his or her family group. Other researchers have observed that the same behavior by a family member can have different connotation among other ethnic groups. Therefore, it is difficult to determine which behavior is more appropriate or adaptive at any given time (McGoldrick, 2005).

Cultural variant theory attempts to explain difference and adaptability. It suggests that beyond their obvious surface differences, Black and White families also differ in terms of adaptive functioning (Perry & Perry, 2006). Research has found that Black families, especially immigrants, have more contact with extended kin than do White families (Nobles, 1978; Olson, 2006; Perry & Perry, 2006); reflect a more authoritarian parenting style (McGoldrick, 1982; Peters, 1981); place more emphasis on cultural heritage (Takyi, 2002); and display a greater inclination to seek help from church and family networks rather than professional helpers (Peterson, 1986).

Parenting, then, should not be examined alone but rather must be examined within a cultural context that includes the social systems that make up the larger environment in which immigrant families live. Such an examination will be facilitated by a theoretical framework that includes social systems theory, ecological theory, and cultural variant theory. Despite strong support for individual theories and models of parenting, considered singly they are insufficient to explain this complex phenomenon (Eckstein, 2000). These theories provide paradigms for those working with immigrant populations on parenting issues. Above all, I encourage immigrant Christians to incorporate biblical principles in their parenting models so that they can enjoy a better life with their families.

# CHAPTER 8

# RELIGION

RELIGION PLAYS A significant role in the lives of many immigrant parents. Many immigrants are more religious than the broader United States population, and many have used their religious orientation to survive difficult times. I talked with several Nigerian Christians and other immigrant parents about their relationships with their children.

Mary said to me, "When you raise them in the ways of God, they will not misbehave. This will guide them in their lives." Victoria said, "I was lucky to raise them in Pentecostal Church. I made sure that they were involved in church activities. My young adults used to be in the choir members, ushers, and the drama club."

Jose spoke about the conflict between his religious values and the behavior his children were exposed to. He cited pants hanging down, ear piercing among young adult males, and pornography as negative influences. "These things must not happen in a Christian home," he said, "especially in Pentecostal families."

Immigrant parents must see prayer as a key to effective parenting. They must teach their children and young adults to pray constantly because prayer will ease their worries and fears, and will bring hope when the situation is hopeless. To raise successful children in America, immigrant parents should teach their children to pray about their personal and spiritual life, and commit everything into God's hands. For example, Jose spoke about setting aside a specific time to pray together with his family, even with his busy schedule. Victoria affirmed that prayer "will empower them to survive all the hurdles and tribulations of this world." Mary recounted an instance when prayer helped her daughter get admitted to medical school.

My own faith in God was established through the Christian doctrines and foundation I received when I was young. I believe it is important to hold on to your faith and apply it when raising your children, especially young adults, and especially during difficult times. I give my parents an enormous amount of credit for how they raised me and my siblings.

In my career and private life in America, I have faced many challenges, and it would have been easy to become hopeless. But God always restored me through prayer—my own, and others on my behalf. I am very lucky to have parents who encourage me with prayer and words of God. I learned from my parents to hold on to my faith in any circumstances.

I have been inspired by the story of Dr. Ben Carson, whose mother prayed earnestly for her children to become successful. Dr. Carson, an African-American, was the first surgeon to successfully separate Siamese twins joined at the head.

I firmly believe that if you want to be a successful parent and you want your children to be successful, you must pray for your children. Prayer has no limit or boundary; it will carry your children throughout their life.

When you notice your children becoming wayward, you need to intercede for them. In fact, don't wait that long. Pray for them even if they seem successful. Raising children is a sacred responsibility. You must realize that you can't do it alone. I have met too many parents who were proactive about their faith before coming to America, but once they arrived, they abandoned their faith. Their children see this, and then they do not have time to serve God.

Many Americans are too corporate, too busy, too sophisticated to serve God. They don't have time to pray for their children, and everybody does what he or she likes. My dear reader, prayer is the secret for staying strong. Parents need to seek the face of God and surrender all to Him. He has promised that He will not fail us.

When worldly people are using your children to torment you, remember to call upon His name because He will not allow you to carry a burden that is too much to bear. I appeal to parents who are Christians to always pray and ask God for help concerning our children. All we need to do is to cast our burden upon Him. Our children should be our joy, and when we feel sad about them, it's time to run to our heavenly father for help (Isaiah 49:25). When your faith is tested and you think your child will never amount to anything, you need to believe in God. When your child seems to be going in the path of destruction, remember the word of God in Acts 16:30-31.

## Education

Many immigrant parents believe that education is the key to success, and as a result they emphasize the value of education with their children. They believe it is important for their children to attend college and excel academically. They tell their children that education must come first and other things must be secondary. They boast about their children when they graduate because they believe that education is a powerful means of moving up the ladder in society. They believe that education will make their girls independent so that no man can oppress them. Proverbs 2:10-11 says, "When wisdom entereth into thine heart, and knowledge is pleasant unto thy soul, discretion shall preserve thee, understanding shall keep thee."

Education is very important, but parents should remember that it is God who gives wisdom, knowledge, and understanding. When parents are eager to see their children go to college and graduate, they must not forget to encourage their children to seek knowledge and wisdom from God. He is the only one who can help them survive the hurdles of life. Children must be taught how to handle life challenges through the word of God.

Immigrant parents with limited education may think they lack the resources to help their children excel in school. But these parents can still communicate their high educational ambitions for their children and be supportive of teachers and school administrators.

When I ask immigrant parents what they like about America, many describe it as a land of opportunity. They are amazed and impressed by the number of colleges in the United States, compared to their home countries. I encourage them to take advantage of scholarships, grants, and loans. I also encourage them to explore the possibility of online education.

# CHAPTER 9

# PARENTING PRACTICES

A LL CHILDREN NEED to be showered with love and attention. Parents need to explain their behavior and use positive reinforcement because it is more effective than punishment. Traditional societies tend to maintain strict standards of obedience and often use punishment to discipline children. A traditional orientation is often reinforced by the values of a religious subculture. For example, many Southeast Asians—Cambodian, Hmong, Lao, Vietnamese—are influenced by Buddhist beliefs.

Although immigrant parents may represent a variety of religious and cultural traditions, they tend to share certain values: group identity, self-discipline, a hierarchical family structure. And of course they are all trying to raise their children in a new environment.

Many immigrant parents feel as though raising children in the United States requires them to compromise their values and beliefs. They see their children becoming acculturated, and they feel like their parental authority has been compromised. How are they supposed to discipline their children? How can they transmit their family values, and preserve their traditional culture?

## Discipline

There are different ways that immigrant parents can discipline their children and young adults in this culture. My advice to parents is that before you do anything, allow God to be the centerpiece. "For it is God who works in you to will and to act according to his good purpose" (Philippians 2:13).

First, parents must set limits in form of simple rules and regulations for children as long as they live under your roof. Setting limits will allow them to become who God wants them to be and will also protect them from peer pressure. Parents should set a specific time for family meetings and provide time to discuss things with their children.

Discipline includes parental monitoring, which involves supervision and communication. A friend of mine told me that he monitors his children "to make sure that they do not go astray. I monitor them because I want them to remain in school." Proverbs 22:6 says, "Teach your children to choose the right path, and when they are older, they will remain upon it." Your responsibility as a parent includes disciplining your children with tender, loving care. As Christians, you must discipline children when they are wrong but in a way that is pleasing to God. In so doing, you will be serving your children, serving the society they are growing into, and serving God.

Another friend told me, "I discipline my children by not giving them what they want when they misbehave." Nowadays, many parents don't spank their children but instead talk to them and try to be more flexible and listen. Parenting practices have changed, even among immigrants. In their home countries, parents had more authority over their adolescent children, but in the United States immigrant parents find themselves more often cast in the role of negotiator, and compromise is the watchword. This is evident in the way some parents communicate with their children.

For example, James said that he used to scream at his children, but now he listens more so that they can express themselves:

> I am a disciplinarian and I used to shout at my young adult children, but since coming to America, I have toned down a lot and became more flexible with them. I found out that when they hear me talk to them with soft voice or low pitch, they listen. I have realized that shouting with young adult children will only aggravate the situation.

Victoria told me that "in Nigeria, if young adults misbehave we spank them, but in the U.S.A. I am more flexible. Now I talk more with them and listen."

MICHAEL O. AKINTAYO PH.D

When you discipline your children, do so with love. Proverbs 13: 24 suggests that if you refuse to discipline your children, it shows that you don't love them. If you love your children, you will be prompt to discipline them.

## Open Communication

In this country, the most effective way to increase family stability is an open communication process. Recent research suggests that open communication is one of the most appropriate ways of maintaining good parent-teen relationships (Ashman-Kirst & Zastrow, 2007).

Many immigrant parents say have changed their communication style since coming to the United States. For those who have not changed, I encourage you to consider your children's feelings and opinions. It is also important to be aware of the legal protection that young adults have in the United States. Many immigrant parents have modified their parenting practices so as not to run afoul of U.S. laws. Some people may view this as concession, but I encourage you make your family bond strong so that you do not feel you have compromised your core beliefs and values as a parent. And beyond what civil law may require, the Bible teaches us that parents should not aggravate their children (Colossians 3:21). If you do, they will become discouraged and quit trying.

## High Moral Standards

It is important to raise your children to respect you as parents, respect their teachers or professors, and respect their elders. The way to do this is by emphasizing high moral standards that are based on your spiritual beliefs, tradition, and culture. You should help your children be committed to their studies and careers, but above all they must obey the doctrines and teachings of God. In the words of Proverbs 3:21, "My son, let not them depart from thine eyes: keep sound wisdom and discretion." Raising your children with proper discipline and instructions from God will ensure that sound values become their foundation for future decisions.

## Becoming Negotiators

As I talk with parents from other cultures, I hear them describe efforts to keep their cultural values, practices, traditions, and language in their host country. Many say they no longer spank their children, but they continue to monitor their behavior. They characterize themselves less as disciplinarians and more as negotiators. Although they do not make this technical distinction, they would probably describe themselves as authoritative rather than authoritarian.

# CHAPTER 10

# EFFECTIVE PARENTING

D EVELOPMENTAL PSYCHOLOGISTS HAVE focused on middle-class and Anglo-European families in examining effective parenting among people of other cultures, and this has resulted in biased results. It is necessary to acknowledge cultural differences in parenting in order to develop practices that will help immigrant parents raise their children in a diverse country like the United States. There are many different ethnic groups in America, and one model should not be a common yardstick to evaluate all effective parenting.

Research on effective parenting has led to typologies of parental styles. Becker (1964) considered the importance of control in maintaining a family system. He favored a democratic system of parental control in producing responsible young adults.

Earlier, Baldwin, Kalhorn, and Breese (1945) observed that democratic parents provide opportunities for children to be involved in family decisions by making sure that rules and decisions are well communicated. These parents are committed to providing their children with a positive self-image and encouraging independence. Autocratic parents, on the other hand, see themselves primarily as the makers and enforcers of rules. Accepting parents emphasize love, warmth, and affection, whereas indulgent parents tend to pamper their children, sometimes showing love and support even when the children are wrong. These parents find it difficult to set high expectations and boundaries for their children.

Baumrind (1989) examined the socialization of children from a broader perspective, proposing that the main goal of parenting is to teach a child to conform to the needs of the family and society while developing self-identity, self-esteem, and honesty. Baumrind suggested that effective parenting is determined by the level of parental control enforced in a family. Control is useful for adjustment and adaptation of individual family members to different situations, which in turn leads to stability of the family as a system.

Baumrind (1989) developed a three-fold typology of parenting styles: authoritative, authoritarian, and permissive. Authoritative parents are controlling but warm and accommodating. Authoritarian parents are controlling and permit only limited individuality and contributions to family decisions. Permissive parents do not control or make demands on their children. Children are allowed to make choices without supervision, and behavior is acceptable even if it is destructive. These parents often provide excuses for their children's behavior and attitudes.

Authoritative parents attempt to direct or monitor their children's actions, but largely through verbal communication. They are willing to explain reasons for rules in order to promote stability in the family system, and they allow individual members to adjust to specific situations or new environments. This parental style is a balance between the authoritarian and permissive styles because it allows parents to monitor their children's activities and gives the children some freedom (Bee & Boyd, 2007). Authoritative parents set reasonable and realistic expectations while demonstrating love and empathy, and they negotiate with their children so the children can understand and comply with rules. Children of authoritative parents tend to be self-motivating, self-actualizing, and self-inspiring (Beger, 2005).

Immigrant parents with strong religious values and beliefs see effective parenting as teaching young adults the way of the Lord: prayer, Bible reading, living a moral and ethical life. Effective parenting includes discipline, even as one acknowledges the need to modify standards to accommodate American cultural norms. Good parents show love and compassion for their children and spend quality time with them.

Many Latino parents I spoke with emphasized that parents teach their children and young adults to have respect for their elders. This value is also affirmed by most Africans. In the Yoruba culture of Nigeria, when children wake up in the morning they go to their parents and greet them. The girls kneel down as a sign of respect, and the boys bow. Respect is closely tied to obedience and staying out of trouble.

Ade is a parent from Nigeria and a Christian who described effective parenting as when young adult children listen to instructions and do what their parents tell them to do. Also, when they stay away from trouble, or when they are not in trouble with the law, and when they are not causing trouble in the family.

Although some immigrants do not see themselves going back to their countries any time soon, they still believe in many traditional parenting methods. However, they also recognize that their children are Americans and will inevitably have an American way of life. They are still strict and tend to treat their children the way they would if they were in their home country. They recognize the need to be proficient in English in order to achieve economic success in the United States, but they are reluctant to give up their language at home. Some parents say the process of acculturation began before they left their countries. Parents began buying their children American-style clothing and allowing them to watch American or European movies before immigrating to the United States.

As a Christian and an immigrant parent, I would sum up effective parenting in America as follows:

1. Children should be instructed in the ways of God.
2. Every household must have rules and regulations, dos and don'ts.
3. Children should be taught to respect their elders.
4. Parents should advise their young adult children about life's important issues.
5. Children's activities and friendships should be monitored.

# CHAPTER 11

# REFLECTIONS

MY OVERRIDING CONVICTION is that child-rearing must be based on prayer and the word of God. This should be a fundamental principle by which immigrant Christians raise their children. My impression is that we must talk more about love, care, and affection as contributing to successful parenting. Every Christian parent should train his or her children to respect them and those who are older. This is the law of God. There is too much freedom for young adults in the United States, and many do not properly respect their elders.

The immigrant parents I have talked with describe many differences between the U.S. and their home countries. Melendez thinks that young adults develop faster in America than in her country. James noted that young adults in the United States enjoy more opportunities to go to college and choose among many disciplines to become who they aspire to be.

It is true that America is a land of many opportunities; however, as Christians we must not lose sight of the fact God admonishes us to pray regarding both good and bad times. Everything in life requires prayer. More so, when we realize that every good thing comes from him. Therefore, it is not too much if we commit our children and young adults into the able hands of God to assist us in raising them to be a blessing to us, to others, and to themselves.

Although immigrant parents see many opportunities for their children in the U.S., they are also aware of disadvantages in this country. Mary talked about how single parenting can affect raising a young adult, while Ade observed that young adults here want to be raised as Americans. He said this causes trouble in families as children demand more freedom from their parents. As I listen to parents, I sympathize with those who feel that in the United States parents are not entrusted with full responsibility for raising their children. Their impression is that most young adults think their parents are too hard on them.

The Bible tells us that when we raise our children with the word of God and they accept that instruction, God promises to multiply their years (Proverbs 4:10-13). Parents, remember that the word of God does not instruct us to do what pleases ourselves. We are to do what is pleasing to God, our creator.

The parents I interviewed described the importance of prayer and how it has helped their families. Mary recounted how her third child prayed for and received a scholarship: "She knows that there is nothing prayer cannot do because she has been raised to understand that." When children from families like this become adults, before they embark on big projects they will first seek the direction from God.

America has given many immigrant parents better opportunities to provide for their children. But as Christians, we must not ignore the negative influence on our children of such things as drugs and lack of respect. Immigrant parents must also realize that because some young adults have to work, by the time they come from school and work, they are tired and want to go to bed. This is why I want to appeal to immigrant parents to modify their household rules so their children can find a balance and avoid unnecessary stress at home.

But there is still a place in every home for discipline, monitoring, supervision, and personal counseling. Mary said, "In the U.S., school kids do whatever they like because teachers fear that they can get in trouble when they discipline a child. In my country it is different." Also, parents should discuss their personal experiences with their children so they can be guided in the right direction.

My dear reader, prayer and discipline are very effective in raising your children and young adults. You may discipline them by not giving them what they want when they misbehave, but make sure you explain the rationale behind your action. Some parents are not used to explaining their actions to their children. Remember, this is the United States, and children want answers to many things. When you make household rules, let them understand how those rules can shape their lives in so many positive ways.

Parents, make sure you create family time and encourage your children to be available for family gatherings and call ahead if they are going to be late. Listen to what Victoria says: "My parenting practices have been very effective because I know what goes on in my children's life. They can confide in me as their mother and sister." James said that his children often change their behavior when he talks to them and prays about it.

On the other hand, sometimes you may feel like my friend Kwame, from Ghana: "The society teaches them that you cannot tell them what to do in America, and as a parent I sometimes end up playing by their rules." Victoria admitted that sometimes her parenting practices are ineffective because her children have busy schedules that prevent them from following her instructions.

The key is to have open communication with your children. Be honest about the situation. Make them feel they are important and show that you care for them; then they can easily talk to you. This last piece of advice may not be easy because to do this you must have their confidence and trust. Your behavior will tell them if they can trust you or not. My prayer is that God will give you the wisdom and understanding to clearly communicate your message to your children.

Many immigrants realize that their parenting styles and practices have changed, despite the fact that they still hold on to some traditional values. I believe there is nothing wrong for parents to be in this kind of situation. Most of the parents I interviewed, described some changes in their parenting since moving to the United States. Taiwo said he is more flexible now, a sentiment echoed by Victoria and James. As parents, we need to show love, care, and compassion when dealing with our children.

Many immigrant parents profess love for America. They are happy to have the resources to take care of their children, compared to their home countries. But they still worry. Koshy, an Asian parent said, "If I was in my country, I would raise them the same way because they have to obey the rules and regulations of the family and move closer to God." Forlenza cited increased pressure from his children to acquire material possessions. He also noted that in his home country, the extended family helps in raising children, more so than in the United States. He added, "We are busier in America than in my country. In the Dominican Republic, I would have more time for my kids."

Philip claimed that his native country has higher moral standards than does the United States. "I love this country, but the standard of

MICHAEL O. AKINTAYO PH.D

raising children or young adults in this country is low." James cited the negative influence of the computer: "Computer chat rooms, My Space, Facebook, and pornography are a bad influence on young adults in this country. When you are not around they will log in and do whatever they want to do." This is the main reason that you as immigrant parent must teach and train your children with the word of God and pray for them daily that God sustain them.

Parenting among immigrants to the United States must be evaluated in light of the varied cultural contexts and social systems that prevail in this country. But above all, parents must look to God as the only sufficient model for their relationship with their children.

# CHAPTER 12

# CONCLUSION

A N OVERRIDING CONVICTION of this book is that religion plays a significant role in the lives of many immigrant parents. Many of the people I talked to described the importance of prayer in their own and their children's lives. Children are taught to put everything before God and to believe that God will guide them in the right direction.

Religion is the basis of moral and ethical instruction. Some immigrant children learn this very early from their parents. They learn to be prayerful and see this as one of the attributes of a true believer. They are taught to bring their supplications before the Lord and expose themselves without any reservations so that their prayers can be answered. As Christians, we must teach our children to be specific when they offer their prayers. To obtain from God, we must avoid mindless repetition or bringing before God irrelevant things. Our children must learn to live a simple but comfortable life. This is the only way that they can have peace of mind.

A major conflict for many immigrant parents is the perceived freedom that young adults have in the United States, compared to their home countries. Too much freedom translates to lack of respect for elders and authority figures. Immigrant parents struggle with how to preserve their culture in the United States. One manifestation of this is whether young adults should speak English at home. Many parent-child conflicts arise from the parents' wish to preserve cultural values (obedience, respect for elders, etc.) clashing with their children's desire to adopt American cultural norms and to be treated as adults. In some respects, though, the concerns of immigrant parents are similar to their native-born counterparts. Like most parents, they worry about peer pressure and the effects of part-time jobs on schoolwork (Chao & Tseng, 2002).

On the other hand, immigrant parents appreciate the educational opportunities available in the United States. Rather than decrying the influence of technology, they say it has enhanced their children's academic experience and made it easier to stay in contact when their young adults are away from home. Acknowledging that children in the United States are forced to grow up faster than they would in their home countries, they believe that the greater independence their children experience here has some benefits.

Most of the parents I talked with have changed their communication style since being in the United States, describing themselves as more open to discussion and negotiating with their young adult offspring. They are more inclined to consider their children's feelings and opinions. They are acutely aware of the legal protection that young adults have in American society, and they have modified their parenting practices so as not to run afoul of U.S. laws. Despite what some might view as concessions, however, many parents affirmed to me that their family bonds have remained strong, and they do not believe that they have compromised their core beliefs and values.

In this book, I have described a range of parenting techniques that represent a blending of traditional beliefs and values with American cultural norms. I have stressed prayer, monitoring, discussion, and personal counseling as effective parenting practices. My interviewees characterize parenting as challenging, frustrating, surprising, and rewarding. While they lament the loss of some support systems they would have enjoyed in their home countries, they express gratitude for government support in this country, especially college tuition grants and loans, and they affirm the value of their religious faith in the parenting enterprise.

In conclusion, I encourage immigrant Christian parents to develop trust in their relationship with their children and young adults. This is one of the ways that you can reach out to them. It is your responsibility to teach and train them to develop and improve their talents. During family time, teach them to develop confidence by showing them that they are important to you, to family and society at large. As parents, I encourage you to always listen to their opinion on issues before passing judgments. You are to respect their views on issues and guide them to make right decisions. Although, you might not have had the opportunity during childhood to verbalize your opinions but times have changed, and relationships are growing better or improving between parents, adults and children.

Immigrant parents must encourage their children and young adults to make their choices by providing them with tools and information needed to be independent. Above all, teach them to seek God's favor and guidance in all they do. When they make mistakes, let them know it's okay to make mistakes and it's part of growing up. Mistakes will eventually allow them to make the right choices or decisions in future. This method will allow them to be in control and allow you to play supportive roles rather than being in control.

In your relationship with your children make sure you are honest with them. Honesty will lead to trust. There is nothing as bad as making your children realize that you are not truthful in your dealings with them. It hurts for a child to find out that his or her parents are lairs. Once they find out, they will never trust you again. Honesty will also gain you respect in your relationship with your children. As parents, be who you are and who God wants you to be in the presence of your children. Know your strengths and weaknesses. Prepare your children and young adults to know that they do not need to imitate anyone. They need to be who they are and who God wants them to be. Remember that Jesus Christ was a son of Joseph the Carpenter but did great things. He did not allow his background to prevent or limit him from accomplishing great things. Teach your children and young adults to appreciate what they have. Teach them to appreciate their potential regardless of their cultural background.

I want to inform you as parents that, it depends on how you raise your children and young adults in the United States that determines who they become in the future. Their racial, cultural and ethnic background can also serve as strengths and not weaknesses alone. There are great men and women of the same diversity who have been successful in this country. As parents, what you demonstrate and teach these children and young adults will remain with them for a very long time.

To all Christian parents and my readers, teach your children and young adult to have the fear of God, create in them the habits of prayer, respect, obedience and love to mankind. Teach them to be grateful or appreciative of what they have, show them how to appreciate others and not to be envious of others in negative ways. Teach them the habit of working towards their dreams and waiting patiently. Let them know

MICHAEL O. AKINTAYO PH.D

that patience is a virtue. Avoid popular culture when you are raising your children in the United States.

To parents, you must continue to learn how to prevent your children and young adults from being influenced by their peers. These qualities will be useful to your children and young adults in their relationships. Finally, pray, pray and pray always for your children and young adults as you raise them in the United States. As Christians, it is the only tool you have to raise them effectively in a country that is tainted with disrespectful children and young adults. Remember that as parents you have the responsibility of raising responsible and productive adults in the United States.

# REFERENCES

Ahmed, S. M., & Lemkau, J. P. (2000). Cultural issues in the primary care of South Asians. *Journal of Immigrant Health, 2*(2), 89-96.

Allen, W. R. (1978). The search for applicable theories of black family life. *Journal of Marriage and the Family, 40,* 117-131.

Andersen, R. E., Carter, I., & Lowe, I. (2006). *Human behavior in the social environment: A social systems approach* (3rd ed.). New York: Aldine Publishing Company.

Ashman-Kirst, K. N., & Zastrow, K. C. (2007). *Understanding human behavior and social environment* (7th ed.). Belmont, CA: Brooks/Cole.

Bacallao, M. L., & Smokowski, P. R. (2007). The costs of getting ahead: Mexican family system changes after immigration. *Family Relations, 56*(1), 52-67.

Bacum, D., Smith, C. D., Kagan, D., & Segal, A. C. (2004). *Psychology: An introduction* (9th ed.). Belmont, CA: Wadsworth/Thomson Learning.

Baldwin, A. L., Kalhorn, J., & Breese, F. (1945). Patterns of parent behavior. *Psychological Monographs, 58*(3), 1-75.

Baumrind, D. (1971). Current patterns of parental authority. *Developmental Psychological Monographs, 4,* 1-103.

Baumrind, D. (1989). Rearing competent children. In N. Damond (Ed.), *Child development, today, and tomorrow* (pp. 349-378). San Francisco: Jossey-Bass.

Becker, W. C. (1964). Consequences of different kinds of parental discipline. In M. L. Hoffman & L. W. Hoffman (Eds.), *Review of child development* (vol. 1). New York: Sage.

Bee, H., & Boyd, R. (2007). *The developing child* (11th ed.). Boston: Ally & Bacon.

Berk, L. E. (2006). *Child development* (7th ed). New York: Ally & Bacon.

Bornstein, M. H. (2005). Parenting matters. *Infant Child Development, 14*(3), 311-314.

Bornstein, M. H., & Cote, L. R. (2004). Who is sitting across from me? Immigrant mothers' knowledge of parenting and children's development. *Pediatrics, 114*(5), 557-564.

Bronfenbrenner, U. (2001). The bioecological theory of human development. In W. Smelser & P. Bates (Eds.), *Introductory encyclopedia of the social and behavioral sciences* (pp. 6963-6970). New York: Elsevier.

Brown, K. A. (2008). The influence of religion, spirituality, and culture on career choices of African American young adults. *Dissertation Abstract International.* (UMI 1452497)

Chao, R., & Tseng, V. (2002). Parenting of Asians. In M. H. Borstein (Ed.), *Handbook of parenting. Vol. 4, applied parenting* (2nd ed., pp. 59-93). Mahwah, NJ: Lawrence Erlbaum.

Christian, M. D., & Barbarian, O. A.(2001). Cultural resources and psychological adjustment of African American children: Effects of spirituality and racial attribution. *Journal of Black Psychology, 27*(1), 43-63.

Corey, G. (2005). *Theory and practice of counseling psychotherapy* (7th ed.). Belmont, CA: Brooks/Cole Thompson Learning.

Dale, O., Smith, R., Norlin, J. M., & Chess, W. A. (2006). *Human behavior and the social environment* (5th ed.). Boston: Allyn & Bacon.

Dixey, R. A. (1999). "Fatalism" accident causation and prevention: Issues for health promotion from an exploratory study in a Yoruba town in Nigeria. *Health Educational Research, 14*(2), 197-208.

Eckstein, K. (2000). Holistic parenting: A comprehensive approach to parenting education. *Dissertation Abstracts International* (UMI 9975595)

Fox, L. A .(2003). The role of the church in the career development in African American college students: A qualitative inquiry. *Career Development Quarterly, 54,* 227-241.

Harkness, S., Super, C. M., & van Tijen, N. (2000). Individualism and the "Western mind" reconsidered: American and Dutch parents' ethnotheories of the child. *New Directions for Child and Adolescent Development, 87*(1), 23-30.

Healey, J. F. (2006). *Race, ethnicity, gender, and class: The sociology of group conflict and change* (4th ed.). Thousand Oaks, CA: Sage.

Herrerias, C. (1988). Prevention of child abuse and neglect in the Hispanic community: The MADRE parent education program. *Journal of Primary Prevention, 9,* 104-119.

Jack, G. (2000). Ecological influences on parenting and child development. *Journal of Social Work, 30,* 703-720.

Kamya, H. (2005). African immigrant families. In M. McGolrick, J. Giordano, & N. Garcia-Preto (Eds.), *Ethnicity and family therapy* (3rd ed.). New York: Guiford Press.

Longress, J. F. (2000). *Human behavior in social environment* (3rd ed.). Victoria: Thompson-Brook Cole.

Martinez, E. A. (1988). Child behavior in Mexican American/Chicano families, maternal teaching, and childrearing practices. *Family Relations*, *37*, 106-119.

McGoldrick, M. (2005). Normal families: An ethnic perspective. In F. Walsh (Ed.), *Normal family national action*. Washington, DC: U.S. Department of Labor, Office of Planning and Research.

Melendez, L. (2005). Parental beliefs and practices around early self-regulation: The impact of culture and immigration. *Infants & Young Children*, *18*(2), 136-146.

Minuchin, P. (2005). Relationships within the family: A systems perspective on development. In R. A. Hinde & J. Stevenson-Hinde (Eds.), *Relationships within families: Mutual influences* (pp. 7-26). Oxford: Oxford Science Publications.

National Campaign, (2008). What research tells us about Latino parenting practices and their relationship to youth sexual behavior. Retrieved 07/10/09 from www.TheNationalCampaign.org

Nobles, W. W. (1978). Toward an empirical and theoretical framework for defining black families. *Journal of Marriage and the Family*, 679-688.

Nobles, W. W. (1980). African philosophy: Foundations for black psychology. In R. Jones (Ed.), *Black psychology* (2nd ed.). New York: Harper & Row.

Ogunnaike, O. (1997). Yoruba toddlers: Relating cognitive performance to family sociodemographic performance and mediating factors in the child's environment. *Dissertation Abstracts International*, *58*(03), 1568B. (UMI No. 9726595)

Oyeshile, O. A. (2003). Traditional Yoruba social-ethical values and governance in modern Africa. *Philosophical Africana*, *6*(2), 81-89.

Osundeko, T. O. (2006). The role of acculturation in child-rearing practices of Nigerian Yoruba Immigrants: A phenomenological study. *Dissertation Abstracts International* [UMI 3213418].

Parke, R. D. (2004). Development in the family. *Annual Review of Psychology, 35*(1), 365-400.

Perry, J. A., & Perry, E. K. (2006). *Contemporary society: An introduction to social science.* Boston: Ally & Bacon.

Porpora, D. V. (1989). Four concepts of social structure. *Journal for the Theory of Social Behavior 19*(2), 195-211.

Riesch, S. K., Anderson, L .S., & Krueger, H. A. (2006). Parent-child communication processes: Preventing children's health-risk behavior. *Journal for Specialists in Pediatric Nursing,* 11(1).

Soyinka-Airewelle, P. (2003). When neutrality is taboo: Navigating institutional identity in protracted conflict settings: The Nigeria Ife/Modakeke case. *African and Asian Studies, 2*(3), 259-306.

Takyi, B. (2002). The making of the second Diaspora: On the recent African-American immigrant community in the USA: *Western Journal of Black Studies, 26,* 32-44.

Veal, M. L., & Ross, L. T. (2004). *Parental monitoring, family dysfunction, and binge drinking.* Unpublished manuscript.

www.ingramcontent.com/pod-product-compliance
Lightning Source LLC
Chambersburg PA
CBHW031328290526
45784CB00014B/2419